Project Management

Get from the idea to implementation successfully

Fourth Edition

Marion E. Haynes

Viva Books
New Delhi | Mumbai | Chennai | Kolkata
Bengaluru | Hyderabad | Kochi | Guwahati

First Indian Edition 2011

VIVA BOOKS PRIVATE LIMITED

- 4737/23 Ansari Road, Daryaganj, New Delhi 110 002
  E-mail: vivadelhi@vivagroupindia.net, Tel. 42242200
- 76, Service Industries, Shirvane, Sector 1, Nerul, Navi Mumbai 400 706
  E-mail: vivamumbai@vivagroupindia.net, Tel. 27721273, 27721274
- Jamals Fazal Chambers, 26 Greams Road, Chennai 600 006
  E-mail: vivachennai@vivagroupindia.net, Tel. 28290304, 28294241
- B-103, Jindal Towers, 21/1A/3 Darga Road, Kolkata 700 017
  E-mail: vivakolkata@vivagroupindia.net, Tel. 22836381, 22816713
- 7, Sovereign Park Apartments, 56-58, K. R. Road, Basavanagudi, Bengaluru 560 004
  E-mail: vivabangalore@vivagroupindia.net, Tel. 26607409, 26607410
- 101-102 Mughal Marc Aptt., 3-4-637 to 641, Narayanguda, Hyderabad 500 029
  E-mail: vivahyderabad@vivagroupindia.net, Tel. 27564481, 27564482
- First Floor, Beevi Towers, SRM Road, Kaloor, Kochi 682 018, Kerala
  E-mail: vivakochi@vivagroupindia.net, Tel: 0484-2403055, 2403056
- 232, GNB Road, Beside UCO Bank, Silpukhuri, Guwahati 781 003
  E-mail: vivaguwahati@vivagroupindia.net, Tel: 0361-2666386

www.vivagroupindia.com

Published by arrangement with

Axzo Press, LLC
562, Willow Brook Office Park
Fairport, New York 14450

ISBN : 978-81-309-1825-9

Published by Vinod Vasishtha for Viva Books Private Limited, 4737/23, Ansari Road, Daryaganj, New Delhi - 110 002. Printed and bound by Raj Press, R-3, Inderpuri, New Delhi - 110 012.

Table of Contents

About the Author

Marion E. Haynes is the author of three titles in the Crisp 50-Minute Series. He has published 35 articles and ten books on management and supervisory practices, as well as retirement and life planning.

Mr. Haynes is a graduate of Arizona State University with a BS degree in Business Administration. He holds the MBA degree, with distinction, from New York University.

He retired from Shell Oil Company in 1991 after a 35-year career in human resource management. At retirement, he was the corporate level manager of pensioner relations. Following retirement, he joined the staff of Price-Waterhouse as a consultant working as a member of a three-person team presenting retirement planning workshops for Price-Waterhouse clients.

Mr. Haynes was appointed an adjunct professor at the University of Houston's College of Continuing Education. He also served as an instructor for the hospitality industry's executive course presented each year by the University's Conrad Hilton College of Hotel and Restaurant Management. He also presented public workshops at several universities in the South-Central U.S.

He served for four years on the board of directors of Sheltering Arms, a social service agency for the elderly in Houston, Texas. During this time, he chaired the agency's personnel committee and served on its executive committee.

He was a member of the board of directors of the International Society for Retirement Planning for eight years, serving as president from 1991 to 1993. He also chaired the editorial board for the society's journal and served on its newsletter board.

Today, he and his wife, Janice, live in Kerrville, Texas, where he pursues his interests in writing, community service, and travel.

Learning Objectives

Complete this book, and you'll know how to:

1) Discuss the basic principles of project management.
2) Define the project to be managed.
3) Plan a project.
4) Implement a project management plan.
5) Complete a project.

Workplace and Management Competencies mapping

For over 30 years, business and industry has utilized competency models to select employees. The trend to use competency-based approaches in education and training, assessment, and development of workers has experienced a more recent emergence within the Employment and Training Administration (ETA), a division of the United States Department of Labor.

The ETA's General Competency Model Framework spans a wide array of competencies from the more basic competencies, such as reading and writing, to more advanced occupation-specific competencies. The Viva-Crisp Series finds its home in what the ETA refers to as the Workplace Competencies and the Management Competencies.

Project Management covers information vital to mastering the following competencies:

Workplace Competencies:

- Planning & Organizing

Management Competencies:

- Informing
- Monitoring Work
- Monitoring & Controlling Resources

About the Viva-Crisp 50-Minute Series

The Viva-Crisp 50-Minute Series was designed to cover critical business and professional development topics in the shortest possible time. Our easy-to-read, easy-to-understand format can be used for self-study or for classroom training. With a wealth of hands-on exercises, the 50-Minute books keep you engaged and help you retain critical skills.

What You Need to Know

We designed the Viva-Crisp 50-Minute Series to be as self-explanatory as possible. But there are a few things you should know before you begin the book.

Exercises

Exercises look like this:

EXERCISE TITLE

Questions and other information would be here.

Keep a pencil handy. Any time you see an exercise, you should try to complete it. If the exercise has specific answers, an answer key is provided in the appendix. (Some exercises ask you to think about your own opinions or situation; these types of exercises don't have answer keys.)

Forms

A heading like this means that the rest of the page is a form:

FORMHEAD

Forms are meant to be reusable. You might want to make a photocopy of a form before you fill it out, so that you can use it again later.

A Note to Instructors

We've tried to make the Viva-Crisp 50-Minute Series books as useful as possible as classroom training manuals. Here are some of the features we provide for instructors:

- PowerPoint presentations
- Answer keys
- Assessments
- Customization

PowerPoint Presentations

You can download a PowerPoint presentation for this book from our Web site at www.CrispSeries.com.

Answer keys

If an exercise has specific answers, an answer key will be provided in the appendix. (Some exercises ask you to think about your own opinions or situation; these types of exercises will not have answer keys.)

Assessments

For each 50-Minute Series book, we have developed a 35- to 50-item assessment. The assessment for this book is available at www.CrispSeries.com. *Assessments should not be used in any employee-selection process.*

PART 1

Project Management Concepts

"Of all the things I've done, the most vital is coordinating the talents of those who work for us and pointing them towards a certain goal."

–Walt Disney

In this part:

- Project Management Basics
- The Project Life Cycle
- Project Parameters
- Project Management Software
- Common Terms and Abbreviations

Project Management Basics

Projects are temporary undertakings that have a definite beginning and end and are carried out to meet established goals within cost, schedule, and quality objectives. Projects are thus distinguished from the ongoing work of an organization. Project management brings together and optimizes the resources necessary to complete the project successfully. These resources include the skills, talents, and cooperative efforts of a team of people; facilities, tools, and equipment; information, systems, and techniques; and money. Project management is equally as effective when applied to projects at home, at school, or in community service.

How Did Project Management Develop?

The concept of project management as a discipline was developed to manage the U.S. space program in the early 1960s. It expanded rapidly into government, the military, and industry. Today you'll find its principles also applied to program management, product management, and construction management.

How Does Project Management Differ from Other Management Principles?

Project management differs in two significant ways. First, while department managers, or managers of other organizational units, expect their organizations to exist indefinitely, project managers focus on an undertaking with a finite lifespan. Second, project managers frequently need resources on a temporary basis, whereas permanent organizations try to utilize resources full-time. The sharing of resources frequently leads to conflict and requires skillful negotiation to see that projects get the necessary resources to meet objectives throughout the life cycle of a project.

"Let's restart this project with a blank slate."

The Project Life Cycle

Each project moves through a predictable life cycle, and each phase of the project calls for different skills from the project manager. The phases of a project life cycle are discussed in this book and include:

- Conceiving and defining the project
- Planning the project
- Implementing the plan
- Completing and evaluating the project

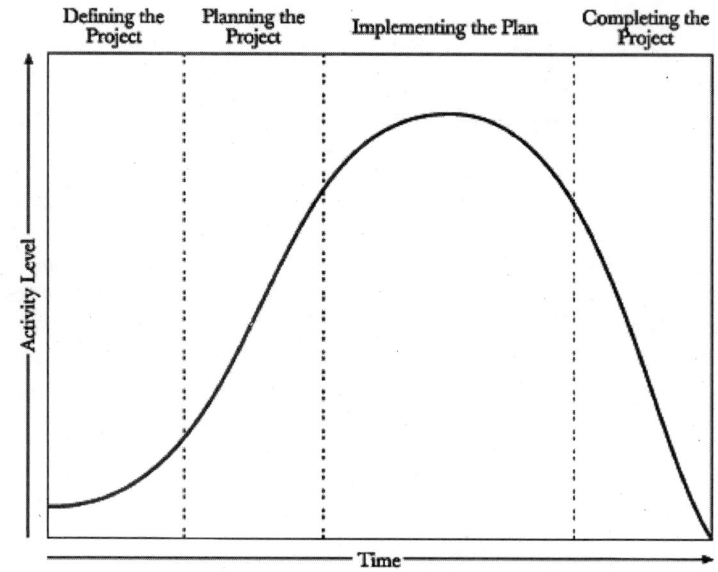

Typical Activity Levels During the Phases of a Project's Life

YOUR PROJECT MANAGEMENT EXPERIENCE

Think of a project you've completed within the last few months. It may have been a weekend project at home or something at work.

Now, respond to the following questions:

1. When did you first get the idea for the project? How much time elapsed and what steps were involved between the idea conception and a clear understanding of what you were going to do?

____

____

____

____

____

____

____

2. How did you go about planning the project? Did you think about what tools, equipment, and supplies you'd need and where to obtain them? Did you arrange for extra help if you couldn't handle the project alone?

____

____

____

____

____

____

____

CONTINUED

CONTINUED

3. Once you got under way, did everything go according to plan? Did you stay within budget? Did you finish on time? Did you meet your quality standards? Did any unanticipated problems occur? If so, how did you deal with them?

____

____

____

____

____

4. When the project was completed, were there people to be released or reassigned, tools and equipment to be returned, or surplus material to be disposed of?

____

____

____

____

____

5. After the project was completed, did you spend any time reflecting on the experience to see where improvements could have been made in the management of the project? If not, take a few minutes now and write down some ideas for improvement.

____

____

____

____

____

Project Parameters

During a project's life, management focuses on these basic parameters:

- Quality
- Time
- Cost

A successfully managed project is one that's completed at the specified level of quality, on or before the deadline, and within budget.

Each of these parameters should be specified in detail during the planning phase of the project. These specifications then form the basis for control during the implementation phase.

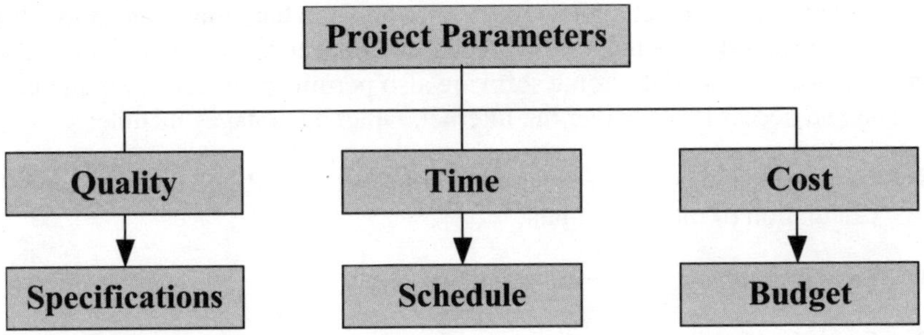

Not every project requires the same attention to each of these activities. Everything depends upon the type of project you're undertaking, its size and scope, and the type of organization you're affiliated with. Use your own judgment in selecting the steps important to the success of your project.

Best of luck in the projects you undertake. Success can be yours if you use the concepts presented here.

Project Management Software

Several good software applications are available to help plan and monitor projects. Some require the purchase of a license; others are open-source. Of these, some install on your hard drive, while others are Web-based. These applications make it much easier to track progress, especially on large, complicated projects. But they can't define projects, set objectives, determine budgets or time requirements. They can't define control points, activities, or relationships. These very important activities must be done by a project manager or team members.

What to Expect from Project Planning Software

The major benefit of project management software is in handling large amounts of data. This type of software makes the preparation of reports and charts both easy to do and professional-looking. Some software also permits project team members to enter data and access reports over the Internet. Other advantages include:

- Easy development and editing of Gantt charts and PERT diagrams and the calculation of the critical path.
- Easy production of schedules and budgets.
- Easy access to project information for preparing reports.
- Integration of a project schedule with a calendar allowing for weekends and holidays.
- Easy access to various scenarios for contingency planning and updating.
- Easy checking for errors in logic and over-scheduling of individuals and groups.

Getting Started

A recent review of available software listed nearly 100 different applications. One of the most popular is Microsoft Project. If you believe a software application would be of benefit, take some time to review the features of the applications that are available. Then, choose the one that best fits your needs.

When you work with project planning software for the first time, it's a good idea to experiment with it using a project you've already completed. This allows you to become familiar with the program before putting it to work.

Common Terms and Abbreviations

Acronym	Meaning
ACWP	Actual Cost of Work Performed
B & P	Bid and Proposal
BAC	Budget at Completion
BCWP	Budgeted Cost of Work Performed
CCN	Contract Change Notice
CDR	Critical Design Review
CFSR	Contract Funds Status Report
CPFF	Cost Plus Fixed Fee
CPIF	Cost Plus Incentive Fee
CPM	Critical Path Method
C/SSR	Cost/Schedule Status Report
EAC	Estimate at Completion
ETC	Estimate to Complete
FP	Fixed Price
G & A	General and Administrative
ODC	Other Direct Cost
PDR	Preliminary Design Review
PERT	Program Evaluation & Review Technique
PM	Project Manager or Management
PO	Purchase Order
PR	Purchase Requisition
RFP	Request for Proposal
RFQ	Request for Quotation
T & M	Time and Material
WBS	Work Breakdown Structure
WO	Work Order

PROJECT MANAGEMENT CONCEPTS

For each of the following statements, check true (T) or false (F).

	T	F
1. Projects have a definable beginning and end.	❑	❑
2. Projects must meet cost, schedule, and quality objectives.	❑	❑
3. Project management is no different from other management.	❑	❑
4. A project has a definable life cycle.	❑	❑
5. Projects are managed on three basic parameters.	❑	❑
6. A successful project need not be completed on time.	❑	❑
7. Activity level is typically greatest during the planning phase.	❑	❑
8. A project's schedule defines its costs.	❑	❑
9. Project management as a discipline developed in the 1850s.	❑	❑
10. Project management has no application outside work.	❑	❑
11. Project management software should be used for all projects.	❑	❑
12. G & A is short for general and administrative expenses.	❑	❑

Compare your answers to those of the author in the Appendix.

Part Summary

In this part, you learned how to discuss the **project life cycle** and the project **parameters**. Next, you learned how to use project management **software**. Finally, you learned common **terms and abbreviations**.

P A R T **2**

Defining the Project

"The single best payoff in terms of project success comes from having good project definition early."

–Rand Corporation

In this part:

- The Origin of Projects
- Getting Underway: Action Items
- Testing Your Preliminary Strategy

The Origin of Projects

Projects grow out of problems or opportunities. At work, they're initiated by upper management, clients, or staff members. At school, they may be initiated by teachers, students, or administrators. At home, you yourself or other family members may start projects. A project is born when someone reacts to the level of frustration surrounding a problem or someone sees an opportunity to move into a new venture. When a decision is made to do something about the problem or opportunity, a project is born—at this point, someone is typically given the responsibility of carrying it out. That person becomes the project manager.

Recognizing and Avoiding Pitfalls

A project's initiator is almost always unclear about some aspects of the project. Project personnel tend to stress their own points of view during the stage of defining and structuring the project. But disaster can result if personal biases and interests are left unchecked. Such disasters can be avoided by full discussion among the project manager, client, and staff at the project's inception. With a clear understanding of what's expected, the project manager is now ready to begin defining the project.

Negotiating Specifications with the Client

If there's a client involved who must accept the project upon completion, the specifications that define a successful outcome must be negotiated and agreed to by the client and included as part of the agreement.

A client may be either internal or external. Also, there may be more than one client, especially when the project is internal to an organization. For example, the case study used throughout this book is a project to construct more workspace. The clients are the department that will use the space, as well as management, both of whom must agree to the budget and schedule.

In the course of a project, specifications may change. The project manager has a responsibility to make sure that the client—whether external or internal—agrees to the revised specifications. If there's a written agreement, it needs to be adjusted, and all involved parties must sign off on it. Doing so ensures that the project team and the client are in agreement on the parameters of success when the final inspection is done.

Getting Underway: Action Items

When the project team is assembled, the first order of business is to clarify the project's definition and scope, as well as the basic strategy for carrying it out. The following sequence describes the action items involved in this process.

1. **Study, discuss, and analyze.** Spend adequate time studying, discussing, and analyzing the project. This establishes a clear understanding of what you're dealing with. Spend time here to ensure that you're addressing the right problem or pursuing the real opportunity.

2. **Write a project definition.** When you're confident that you have a firm grasp of the situation, work up a preliminary project definition. This preliminary definition is subject to revision as additional information and experience is acquired.

3. **Set an end-results objective.** Using the project definition, state the end-results objective to be met at the project's conclusion.

4. **List imperatives and desirables.** List the outcomes that must be met for the project to be considered successful. Then list the desirable outcomes that are nonessential but would enhance the project's success. Some project managers refer to these as the "must-haves" and the "nice-to-haves."

5. **Generate alternative strategies.** Now you're ready to generate alternatives that might lead you to your objective. To generate alternatives, try brainstorming with your team.

6. **Evaluate alternatives.** Next, evaluate the alternative strategies you generated. Be sure that your criteria for evaluation are realistic and reflect the end-results objective.

7. **Choose a course of action.** Evaluation allows you to choose a course of action that meets both your project definition and end-results objectives.

Good Objectives Are SMART

In fulfilling the third action item—setting an end-results objective—it's important to know the elements that make up a good objective. The SMART acronym will help you craft your objective. Remember that a SMART objective is:

S **pecific.** A good objective says exactly what you want to accomplish.

M **easurable.** Being specific helps make your objective measurable.

A **ction-oriented.** When writing objectives, use statements that have active verbs and are complete sentences.

R **ealistic.** Good objectives must be attainable yet present a challenge.

T **ime-limited.** Set a specific time by which to achieve the objective.

"Whatever you do, don't mention the 'Mars Project' to him."

WRITE AN OBJECTIVE

Write an objective for a project you may be responsible for. Example*:* Complete landscaping by May 31, at a cost not to exceed $2,500.00.

Brainstorming to Generate Alternatives

Brainstorming is a free-form process that taps the creative potential of a group through association of ideas. Association works as a two-way current: When a group member voices an idea, this stimulates ideas from others, which in turn leads to more ideas from the one who initiated the idea. Follow these guidelines:

- List all ideas offered by group members.
- Don't evaluate, judge, or discuss ideas except to clarify understanding.
- Welcome "blue sky" ideas. It's easier to eliminate ideas later.
- Repetition is okay. Don't waste time sorting out duplication.
- Encourage quantity. The more ideas you generate, the greater your chance of finding a useful one.

Choosing among Alternatives

Consensus is an effective way to choose among alternatives. It isn't the same as complete unanimity. However, everyone should be able to accept the group's decision on the basis of logic and feasibility. When everyone feels this way, you've reached a consensus. Here are some guidelines to achieve consensus:

- **Avoid arguing for your position.** Present your position as lucidly and logically as possible, but also consider the input of others. Don't change your mind simply to avoid conflict.
- **Don't assume that someone must win and someone must lose** when discussions reach a stalemate. Instead, look for the next-most acceptable alternative for all parties.
- **Be skeptical of an easy answer.** When agreement seems to come too quickly and easily, think further. Explore the reasons for the agreement and be sure everyone accepts the solution for basically similar or complementary reasons.
- **Avoid conflict-reducing techniques** such as voting, averaging, and bargaining.
- **Differences of opinion are natural** and to be expected. Disagreements can help the group's decision. With a wide range of information and opinions, there's a greater chance that the group will hit upon the best solution.

Testing Your Preliminary Strategy

Before moving to a full-scale project, a feasibility study should be carried out to test your preliminary strategy and answer the basic question, "Will it work?" Depending on the nature of the project, there are several methods to help answer this question. The choices are to do a *market study,* a *pilot test,* or a *computer simulation*.

The amount of money and other resources that are invested in feasibility studies must be in proportion to the amount of money that the project will put at risk. For example, a company that's planning to invest $450 million to retool a factory to manufacture a new appliance will probably consider a $250,000 market study an excellent investment, if it clarifies the design of the appliance before the major investment is made. On the other hand, a franchised cookie company that's planning to add a new kind of cookie to its line can simply mix up a batch at one store, sell them for a week, and look at sales results—all for a modest investment in local advertising and special ingredients.

Market Study

If your project is to bring a new product to market, you must determine its market potential. Market research asks customers whether your product satisfies their current or potential perceived needs. You can also examine similar products to determine how your product is different from those that are currently available.

Pilot Test

A pilot test is a small-scale tryout of your project. It could be a limited-area market test of a product or a working model of a construction project. Sometimes referred to as "field testing," a pilot test gives you the opportunity to observe your project's performance under actual conditions.

Computer Simulation

Many types of projects can be modeled on computers. For example, the market potential of a product can be predicted by analyzing demographic data of the target users along with certain assumptions about current and potential needs. The load-bearing potential of buildings, bridges, and vessels are analyzed through mathematical calculations.

Computer simulation is used in such diverse fields as aerodynamics, thermodynamics, optical design, and mechanical design. In some cases, the computer is used to assist with the actual design of the project. The major purpose of simulation is to identify potential problems before the project is underway.

Using the Study Results

If the results of a well-conceived and well-executed feasibility study indicate that the project should proceed, you can move confidently into detailed planning and implementation. If the results are discouraging, the data should be used to do a project redesign, followed by another feasibility study, and so on until a successful project concept is identified.

USING THE STUDY

For projects you've work on, how have feasibility studies been performed?

____

____

____

When would a market study be appropriate?

____

____

____

When would a pilot test be appropriate?

____

____

____

When would a computer simulation be appropriate?

____

____

____

When would a feasibility study *not* be appropriate?

____

____

____

Part Summary

In this part, you learned how to discuss the **origin** of projects. Next, you learned how to get underway with **action items** and **objectives**. You learned to **brainstorm** and choose **alternatives**. Finally, you learned how to **test** your **preliminary strategy**.

PART 3

Planning the Project

> ***"Project managers function as bandleaders who pull together their players—each a specialist with individual score and internal rhythm. Under the leader's direction, they all respond to the same beat."***
>
> **–L.R. Sayles**

In this part:

- Planning the Three Project Dimensions
- Planning the Quality Dimension
- Planning the Time Dimension
- Planning the Cost Dimension
- Assigning Responsibility

Planning the Three Project Dimensions

Planning is crucial in project management. Planning means detailing what's required to complete the project successfully along the three critical dimensions:

- ▶ Quality
- ▶ Time
- ▶ Cost

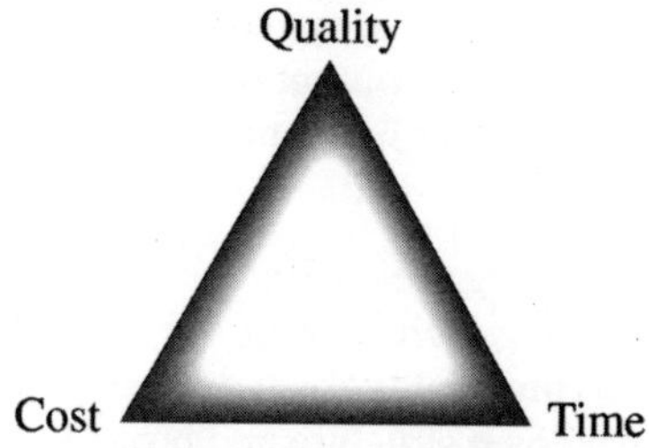

Each of these dimensions is considered in the following pages, along with a variety of tools and techniques for tracking them and ensuring that associated goals are met.

Planning Steps

- ❑ Establish the project objective.
- ❑ Choose a basic strategy for achieving the objective.
- ❑ Break the project into logical steps or subunits.
- ❑ Determine the performance standards for each step.
- ❑ Determine the time required to complete each step.
- ❑ Determine the proper sequence for completing the steps or subunits and aggregate this information into a schedule for the total project.
- ❑ Determine the cost of each step and aggregate costs into the project budget.
- ❑ Design the necessary staff organization, including the number and kind of positions and the duties and responsibilities of each.
- ❑ Determine what training, if any, is needed for project team members.
- ❑ Develop the necessary policies and procedures.

Planning the Quality Dimension

Planning for quality requires attention to detail. The goal of quality planning is to assure that the output of the finished project does what it's supposed to do. A quality plan also establishes the criteria by which the project output is evaluated when the project is finished.

In planning the qualitative dimension, include specifications for the quality and types of materials to be used, the performance standards to be met, and the means of verifying quality, such as testing and inspection. Two techniques—a work breakdown structure and project specifications—facilitate planning for quality. Both are described on the next few pages.

Creating a Work Breakdown Structure

A work breakdown structure (WBS) is the starting place for planning the three project dimensions: quality, cost, and time. The technique divides a project into steps or units of work to be completed in a sequence. Because all elements required to complete the project are identified, a WBS reduces the chances of neglecting or overlooking an essential step.

A WBS is typically configured with two or three levels of detail, although more levels may be required for very complex projects. Start by identifying logical subdivisions of the project, and then break down each of these, thereby adding the second level. As you construct a WBS, keep in mind that the goal is to identify distinct units of work that advance the project toward its completion.

Project management software can produce a WBS from data you enter into the application.

"A project must be broken down into its basic components before you can realistically develop the specifications, budget, and schedule to complete each subunit of work."

–Anonymous

CASE STUDY: WBS

Project: Remodel Building 7 to add four new offices by the end of the third quarter at a cost not to exceed $40,000.

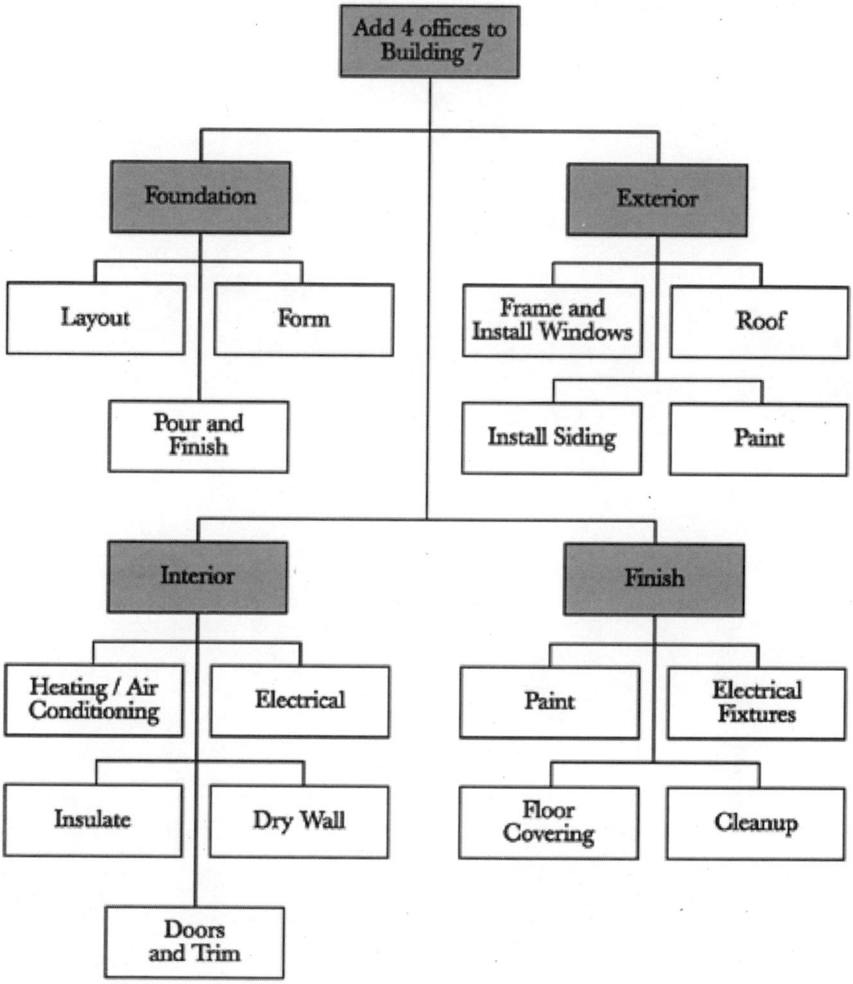

PRACTICE MAKING A WBS

Draw a WBS showing relationships among the steps of the project you're planning.

Project Specifications

From the WBS, specifications can be written for each step of the project. Specifications include everything necessary to meet the project's quality dimension, including materials to be used, standards to be met, tests to be performed, and so on. Use extreme care in writing specifications, because they become the controlling factor in meeting project performance standards. They also directly affect both budget and schedule.

Example of Project Specifications: Foundation

- Pour 4-inch concrete slab over 6 inches of compacted sand fill. Reinforce with 6-by-6-inch, No. 6 wire mesh. Install 6 mil polyethylene membrane waterproofing barrier between sand and concrete.
- Use 1-foot-wide-by-1-foot-long-by-6-inch-deep beams around perimeter of foundation and under load-bearing walls, per blueprints. Beams to include No. 5 reinforcing steel bars in each corner positioned with three stirrups on 2-feet-by-6-inch centers.
- Concrete to withstand 2500 psi test after 28 days.

SPECIFICATIONS EXERCISE

Write specifications for at least one step of the project for which you made a WBS.

Planning the Time Dimension

When planning the time dimension, the objective is to determine the shortest time necessary to complete the project. Begin with the WBS and determine the time necessary to complete each step or subunit. Next, determine the sequence in which steps must be completed, and which steps can be underway simultaneously. From this analysis, you'll determine the three most significant time elements:

- The duration of each step
- The earliest time at which a step may be started
- The latest time by which a step must be started

Planning the time dimension can be done only by people who have experience with the activities designated for each step. If you personally don't know how long it takes to do something, you need to rely on someone who does have the requisite experience.

Many project managers find it realistic to estimate time intervals as a range rather than as a precise amount. Another way to deal with the lack of precision in estimating time is to use a commonly accepted formula for a task. If you're working with a mathematical model, you can determine the probability of the work being completed within the estimated time by calculating a standard deviation of the time estimate.

PLANNING THE TIME REQUIRED

When you're involved with a project, how do you estimate the time required for its completion?

____

____

____

____

____

____

____

Using a Mathematical Model to Estimate Time

T_m—The most probable amount of time necessary to complete the project.

T_o—The optimistic (shortest) time, within which only 1% of similar projects are completed.

T_p—The pessimistic (longest) time, within which 99% of similar projects are completed.

T_e—The calculated time estimate.

$$T_e = \frac{T_o + 4T_m + T_p}{6}$$

σ = Standard deviation

$$\sigma = \frac{T_p - T_o}{6}$$

The work will be completed within the range of $T_e \pm 1$ standard deviation or 68.26% of the time.

The work will be completed within the range of $T_e \pm 2$ standard deviations or 95.44% of the time.

The work will be completed within the range of $T_e \pm 3$ standard deviations or 99.73% of the time.

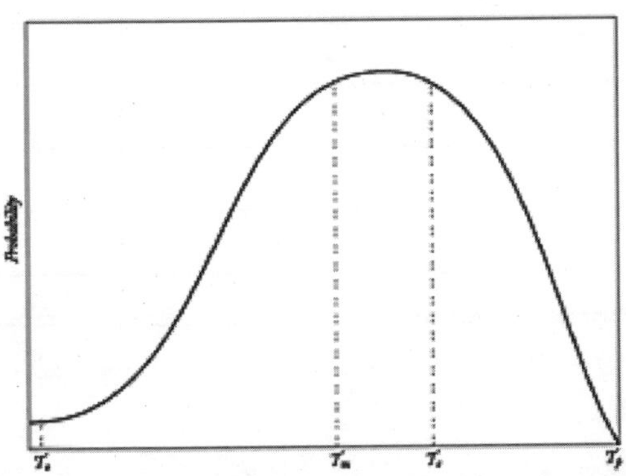

With a duration set for each subunit, the next step is to determine the earliest and latest times for starting each one. Gantt charts and PERT diagrams are two methods commonly used to chart a project. Both are discussed in the pages that follow.

Practice Estimating Time

For the same project that you've been using, determine a time estimate for each of the project's subunits or steps.

Subunit or Step	T_o	T_p	T_m	T_e

Gantt Chart

A Gantt chart is a horizontal bar graph that displays the time relationship of steps in a project. It's named after Henry Gantt, the industrial engineer who introduced the procedure in the early 1900s. Each step is represented by a line placed in the time period during which it's to be undertaken. When completed, a Gantt chart shows a sequential flow of activities, as well as activities that can be underway at the same time.

Example of a Gantt Chart

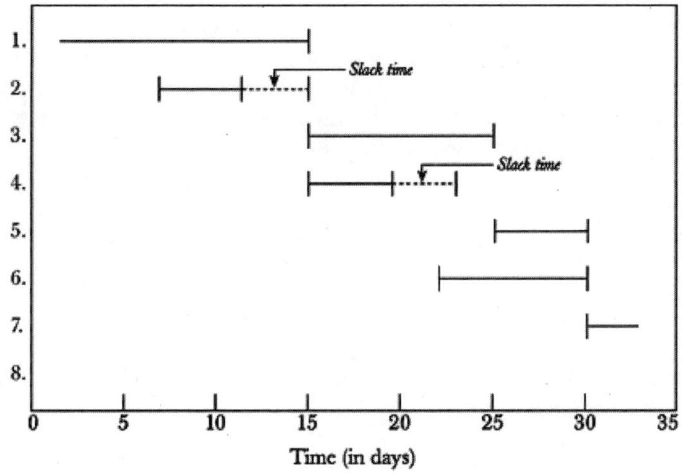

To create a Gantt chart:

1. Determine the steps required to complete a project and estimate the time required for each.
2. List the steps on the left axis of the chart and list the time intervals along the bottom.
3. Draw a horizontal line next to each step, starting at the planned beginning time for the step and ending on its completion time.

Some parallel steps can be carried out at the same time, even when one takes longer than the other. This allows some flexibility on when to start the shorter step; the start time is movable as long as the step is finished in time to flow into subsequent steps. This situation can be shown with a dotted line denoting potential slack time drawn out to the time when the step must be completed.

When your Gantt chart is finished, you can see the minimum total time for the project, the proper sequence of steps, and which steps can be underway at the same time.

Project management software can produce a Gantt chart from data you enter into the application.

Benefits

You can add to the usefulness of a Gantt chart by also charting actual progress. This is usually done by drawing a line in a different color below the original line to show the actual start and finish dates for each step. Doing so allows you to make a quick assessment of whether or not the project is on schedule.

Drawbacks

Gantt charts are limited in their ability to show the interdependencies of activities. In projects where the steps flow in a simple sequence of events, Gantt charts can portray adequate information for project management. However, when several steps are underway at the same time and a high level of interdependency exists among the various steps, PERT diagrams are a better choice.

GANTT CHART USAGE

With projects you've been involved in recently, when do you think a Gantt Chart would have been helpful?

CASE STUDY: Remodeling Project

Project: Remodel Building 7 to add four new offices by the end of the third quarter at a cost not to exceed $40,000. The numbers on the left side of the Gantt chart correspond to the project steps listed below.

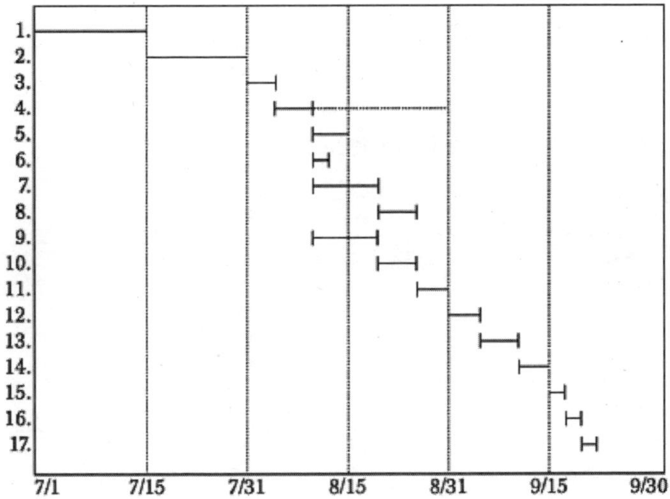

Project Steps, with Time Estimates

1. Complete working plans	15	10. Install heating/AC	5
2. Obtain building permit	16	11. Install insulation	**5**
3. Pour foundation	5	12. Install sheetrock	5
4. Frame walls/roof	5	13. Install doors/trim	5
5. Install roofing	5	14. Paint interior	3
6. Frame/install windows	1	15. Install electrical fixtures	2
7. Install exterior siding	10	16. Clean up	3
8. Paint exterior	3	17. Install floor covering	2
9. Install electrical wiring	10		

Practice Drawing a Gantt Chart

Using the project for which you prepared a WBS, estimate the time required for each step. Then draw a Gantt chart for the project.

Project: ____

____

Project Steps, with Time Estimates

(Total time: ____________)

Step	Time

Step	Time

Gantt Chart

PERT Diagrams

PERT stands for Program Evaluation and Review Technique. It's a more sophisticated form of planning than a Gantt chart and is appropriate for projects with many interactive steps. A PERT diagram has three components:

- Events are represented by circles.
- Activities are represented by arrows connecting the events.
- Non-activities connecting two events are shown as dotted-line arrows. (A non-activity represents a dependency between two events for which no work is required.)

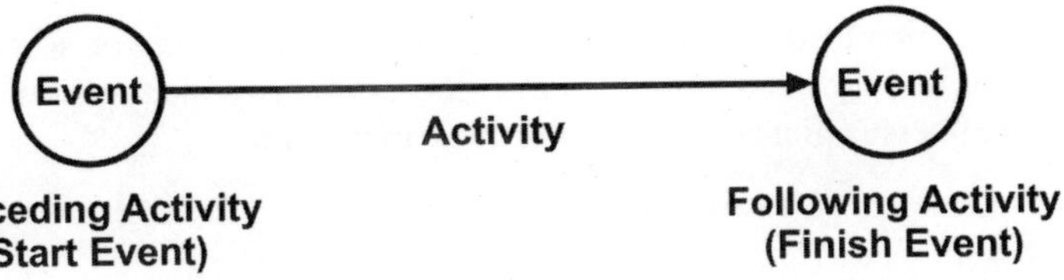

PERT diagrams are most useful if the amount of time scheduled for completing an activity is included on the activity line. Time is recorded in a unit appropriate to the project; days are most common, but hours or weeks can be used. Some diagrams show two numbers: a high estimate and a low estimate.

The most sophisticated PERT diagrams are drawn on a time scale, with the horizontal projection of connecting arrows drawn to represent the amount of time required for each activity. In the process of diagramming to scale, some connecting arrows are longer than completion of that task requires. This represents slack time in the project and is depicted by a heavy dot at the end of the appropriate time period, followed by a dotted-line arrow pointing to the following event.

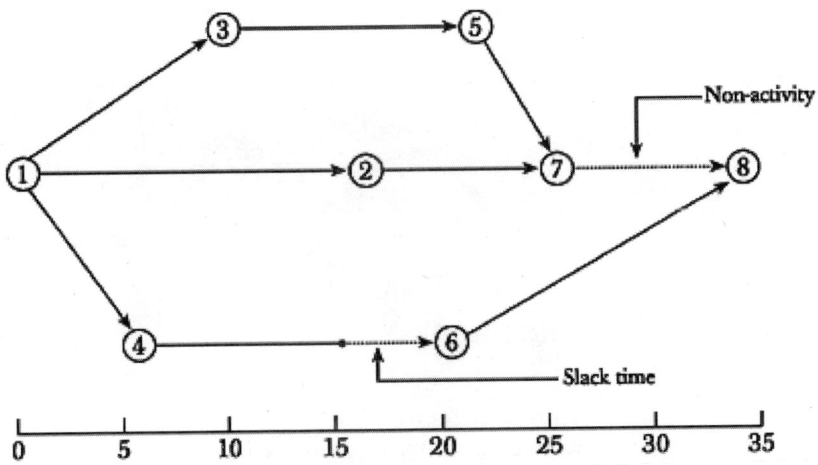

PERT Diagram Drawn to Time Scale

To draw a PERT diagram, list the steps required to finish a project and estimate the time required to complete each step. Then draw a network of relationships among the steps, keeping in mind the importance of proper sequencing. Numbers corresponding to the steps on your list are written in appropriate event circles to identify each step. The time to complete the next step is shown on the arrow. Steps that can be underway at the same time are shown on different paths. Be sure to include all the elements from your WBS.

A PERT diagram not only shows the relationships among various steps in a project but also serves as an easy way to calculate the critical path. The critical path is the longest path through the network and, as such, identifies essential steps that must be completed on time to avoid delays in completing the project. The critical path is shown as a heavy line in the following example.

The usefulness of a PERT diagram can be increased by coloring each step as it's completed. Actual time can be written over the estimated time to maintain a running tally of actual versus planned time along the critical path.

Project management software can produce a PERT diagram from data you enter into the application.

"We were just here for a brainstorming meeting. Please say you did not throw away the napkins."

CASE STUDY: Remodeling Project

Project: Remodel Building 7 to add four new offices by the end of the third quarter at a cost not to exceed $40,000.

Numbers in the circles correspond to the steps listed below. Numbers on the lines show the days required to complete the step that follows.

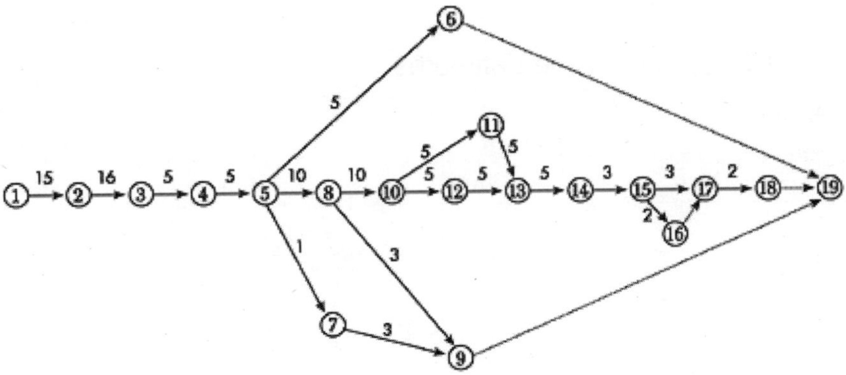

Project Steps, with Time Estimates (in days)

Step	Days
1. Project started	—
2. Working plans completed	15
3. Building permit obtained	16
4. Foundation poured	5
5. Walls/roof framed	5
6. Roofing completed	5
7. Windows installed	1
8. Exterior siding installed	10
9. Exterior painted	3
10. Electrical wiring in	10
11. Heating/air conditioning in	5
12. Insulation installed	5
13. Sheetrock hung	5
14. Interior doors/trim installed	5
15. Interior painted	3
16. Electrical fixtures installed	2
17. Cleanup completed	3
18. Floor covering installed	2
19. Project completed	—

PRACTICE DRAWING A PERT DIAGRAM

Using the project for which you prepared a WBS, estimate the time required for each step. Then draw a Gantt chart for the project.

Project: ____

Project Steps, with Time Estimates

(Total time: ______________)

Step	Time

Step	Time

PERT Diagram

Planning the Cost Dimension

There are many reasons to plan carefully for project costs. To begin with, if you overestimate costs you may lose the job before you begin, because your rates aren't competitive. A good plan includes identifying sources of supplies and materials, and this research helps assure that estimated costs are realistic. The main function of a good budget is to monitor the costs of a project while it's in progress and to avoid cost overruns.

Some inaccuracies in a budget are inevitable, but they shouldn't be the consequence of insufficient attention while drafting the original plan. The goal is to be as realistic as possible.

You can't estimate the cost of your project until you know how long it will take, since labor is typically the most significant cost item. Therefore, use your WBS and project schedule as the starting point for developing your project budget.

Typical costs components include:

- Labor
- Overhead
- Materials
- Supplies
- Equipment rental
- General and administrative
- Profit (if applicable)

Cost Components

- **Labor**: The wages paid to all staff working directly on the project for the time spent on it.
- **Overhead**: The cost of payroll taxes and fringe benefits for everyone working directly on the project for the time spent on it. Usually calculated as a percentage of direct labor cost.
- **Materials**: The cost of items purchased for use in the project. Includes such things as lumber, cement, steel, nails, screws, rivets, bolts, and paint.
- **Supplies**: The cost of tools, equipment, office supplies, and so on that are needed for the project. If something has a useful life beyond the project, its cost should be prorated.
- **Equipment rental**: The cost of renting equipment—such as scaffolding, compressors, cranes, bulldozers, and trucks—for use on the project.
- **General and administrative**: The cost of management and support services—such as purchasing, accounting, and secretarial—for time dedicated to the project. Usually calculated as a percentage of project cost.
- **Profit**: In a for-profit project, the reward to the firm for successfully completing the project. Usually calculated as a percentage of project cost.

With the cost components identified and the project broken down into steps, create a worksheet to tally the costs for the total project.

The cost of a step or subunit is sometimes simplified if it's to be subcontracted. The cost includes bidding the work, selecting a contractor, and then using the contract price as your cost.

Project management software can produce a project budget from your data.

Potential Budget Problems

- The impact of inflation on long-term projects
- The impact of currency exchange rates on international projects
- Failure to obtain firm price commitments from suppliers and subcontractors
- Poorly prepared work breakdown structures that lead to incomplete budgets
- "Fudge factors" built into internal support group estimates
- Estimates based on various methods of cost analysis, e.g., hours versus dollars

CASE STUDY: Remodeling Project

Project Cost Worksheet
(Prepared by general contractor)

Step	Labor	Overhead	Materials	Supplies	Equipment Rental	Gen & Admin	Profit	Total
1. Complete working plans	800	320		200		52.80	274.56	1,647.36
2. Obtain building permit	200	80				11.20	58.24	349.44
3. Pour foundation	2,600	1,040	1,800	200	200	233.60	1,214.72	7,288.32
4. Frame walls/roof	700	420	900			80.80	420.16	2,520.96
5. Install roofing	900	360	1,400			106.40	553.28	3,319.68
6. Frame/install windows	800	320	1,200	50	300	106.80	555.36	3,332.16
7. Install exterior siding	800	320	1,400			100.80	524.16	3,144.96
8. Paint exterior	400	160	220	50	250	43.20	224.64	1,347.84
9. Install electrical wiring	600	240	700			61.60	320.32	1,921.92
10. Install heating/AC	1,400	560	1,800			150.40	782.08	4,692.48
11. Install insulation	300	120	600			40.80	212.16	1,272.96
12. Install sheetrock	800	320	400			60.80	316.16	1,896.96
13. Install doors/trim	320	128	1,400			73.92	384.38	2,306.30
14. Paint interior	400	160	250			32.40	168.48	1,010.88
15. Install electrical fixtures	200	80	650			37.20	193.44	1,160.64
16. Cleanup	300	120	50			18.80	97.76	586.56
17. Install floor covering	240	96	1,400			69.44	361.09	2,166.53
Total	11,760	4,844	14,170	500	750	1,280.96	6,660.99	39,965.95

PRACTICE ESTIMATING PROJECT COSTS

Prepare a cost estimate for the project you've been using. Use as many of the cost columns as apply.

Subunit or step	Labor	Overhead	Materials	Supplies	Equip. Rental	Gen. & Admin	Profit
Total							

Assigning Responsibility

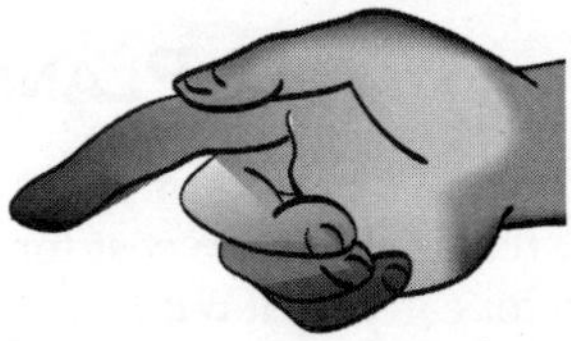

Determining who has responsibility for completing each step of a project should be done as early as possible, so that the leaders can participate in planning schedules and budgets. Participation leads to a greater commitment to achieve the project within time and cost limitations.

The number of people involved in a project varies with its size and scope. Sometimes one person is responsible for more than one step.

To make the best use of your resources when deciding who's responsible for a portion of your project, broaden your point of view to include subcontractors and service departments, as well as project team members.

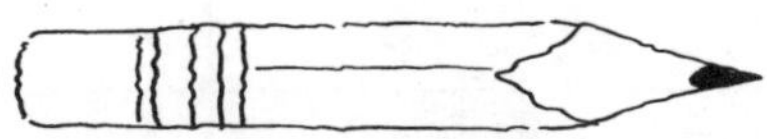

ASSIGN RESPONSIBILITY

With projects you've worked on, how clear were the areas of responsibility?

____

____

____

How did those involved with the project help determine areas of responsibility?

____

____

____

When is it appropriate not to assign responsibilities?

____

____

____

A PLANNING SUMMARY WORKSHEET

Select a project, break it down into its steps or subunits, estimate the time required and the cost for each unit, and identify the person or group responsible for carrying it out.

Project: ____

Component or Step	Budget	Schedule	Responsibility

Part Summary

In this part, you learned how to plan the **three project dimensions**. You learned how to plan the **quality**, **time**, and **cost** dimensions. Finally, you learned how to **assign responsibility** for each step in a project.

PART 4

Implementing the Plan

> *"Do not repeat the tactics which have gained you one victory, but let your methods be regulated by the infinite variety of circumstances."*
>
> –**Sun Tzu**, ***The Art of War***

In this part:

- The Implementation Phase
- Establishing Standards
- Monitoring Performance
- Taking Corrective Action
- Providing Feedback
- Negotiating for Resources
- Ten Guidelines for Effective Negotiation
- Resolving Differences
- Communicating

The Implementation Phase

During the implementation phase, the project manager coordinates all project elements. Responsibilities include controlling work in progress to see that it's carried out according to plan; providing feedback to the team working on the project; negotiating for resources; and resolving differences among those involved with the project. These responsibilities require a variety of skills. This part presents tools and techniques to help project managers during the implementation stage.

There are four key duties during implementation:

1 **Controlling work in progress..**

2 **Providing feedback..**

3 **Negotiating for resources.**

4 **Resolving differences.**

Controlling Work in Progress

Control is the central activity during implementation. The most important tool in this process is the plan that was developed to define the project parameters for specifications, schedule, and budget. These are the standards against which performance is measured. Control involves three steps, each of which is discussed in detail in the pages that follow:

1. Establishing standards
2. Monitoring performance
3. Taking corrective action

Establishing Standards

Standards for the project were set in the project specifications created as part of the planning stage. The project manager must constantly refer to these specifications and make sure the project team is also referencing them. If the project deviates from the original specifications, there's no guarantee that the success predicted by the feasibility studies will actually happen, and the product or project outcome might fail to meet performance standards.

A number of tools are available to help project managers control the project and make sure that the parameters defined in the specifications for quality, time, and budget are actually being met. A Gantt chart or PERT diagram developed at the planning stage is a great device for tracking how the time dimension of the project is proceeding in relationship to the plan.

In the following pages, you'll learn about four additional charts that are useful for project control:

- Control Point Identification Charts
- Project Control Charts
- Milestone Charts
- Budget Control Charts

Control Point Identification Charts

A helpful technique for controlling a project is to invest some time thinking through what's likely to go wrong in each of the three project parameters. Then identify when and how you'll know that something is amiss and what you'll do to correct the problem if it occurs. Doing so helps minimize the likelihood that you'll be caught by surprise, as well as saving time in responding to the problem. A control point identification chart is an easy way to summarize this information.

Example of a Control Point Identification Chart

Control Element	What is Likely to Go Wrong?	How and When Will I Know?	What Will I Do About It?
Quality	Workmanship might be less than desired.	Upon personal inspection of each project stage.	Have substandard work redone.
Cost	Cost of any subunit may exceed budget.	When purchase agreements are made.	Seek alternate suppliers; then consider alternate materials.
Time	Time for any step may exceed schedule.	By closely monitoring actual progress against scheduled critical path.	Improve efficiency; try to capture time from later steps; authorize overtime.

MAKE A CONTROL POINT IDENTIFICATION CHART

Select a project and think through each of the questions relating to the three project parameters.

Project: ____

Control Element	What is Likely to Go Wrong?	How and When Will I Know?	What Will I Do About It?
Quality			
Cost			
Time			

Project Control Charts

Another helpful tool is a project control chart, which uses budget and schedule plans to give a quick status report of the project. It compares actual to planned, calculates a variance on each subunit completed, and tallies a cumulative variance for the project.

To prepare a project control chart, refer to the work breakdown and list all subunits or steps for the project. Then, use the schedule to list the time planned to complete each step, and use the budget to list the expected cost of each step.

As each step is completed, record its actual time and actual cost. Calculate variances and carry the cumulative total forward.

This technique can be put into a spreadsheet on your personal computer. Large projects within a company may be able to use the company's computerized accounting system to create a report that uses cost and schedule data routinely captured for other purposes.

Project management software can produce time and cost variance reports from data you enter into the application.

PROJECT CONTROL CHARTS

With projects you've worked on, how have Project Control Charts been used?

What opportunity do you see to use Project Control Charts?

CASE STUDY: Remodeling Project

Project Control Chart

Project: Remodel Building 7 to add four new offices by the end of the third quarter at a cost not to exceed $40,000

	Cost				Schedule			
Project Steps	**Budget**	**Actual**	**Variance**	**Total**	**Planned**	**Actual**	**Variance**	**Total**
1. Complete working plans	1,600	1,650	50	50	15	15	—	—
2. Obtain building permit	350	350	—	50	16	15	(1)	(1)
3. Pour foundation	7,000	7,200	200	250	5	3	(2)	(3)
4. Frame walls/roof	650	700	50	300	5	5	—	(3)
5. Install roofing	3,400	3,300	(100)	200	5*	6	1	(3)
6. Frame/install windows	3,400	3,300	(100)	100	1*	1	—	(3)
7. Install exterior siding	3,200	3,150	(50)	50	10	9	(1)	(4)
8. Paint exterior	1,400	1,300	(100)	(150)	3			
9. Install electrical wiring	2,000				10*			
10. Install heating/AC	4,700				5			
11. Install insulation	1,300				5			
12. Install sheetrock	1,900				5			
13. Install doors/ trim	2,400				5			
14. Paint interior	1,000				3			
15. Install electrical fixtures	1,200				2			
16. Cleanup	600				3			
17. Install floor covering	2,200				2			
18. Project completion (Total)	38,300				84			

*Not on critical path—excluded from total.

Note: If you prefer over-budget and schedule amounts to be negative numbers, subtract actual from budget and planned. Under-budget and schedule amounts will then be positive numbers.

Project Control Chart

Project Steps	Cost				Schedule			
	Budget	Actual	Variance	Total	Planned	Actual	Variance	Total

Milestone Charts

A milestone chart presents a broad-brush picture of a project's schedule and control dates. It lists those key events that are clearly verifiable by others or that require approval before the project can proceed. If this is done correctly, a project won't have many milestones. Because of this lack of detail, a milestone chart isn't very helpful during the planning phase when more information is required. However, it's particularly useful in the implementation phase, because it provides a concise summary of progress that has been made.

Project management software can produce a milestone chart from data you enter into the application.

Example of a Milestone Chart

Milestone	Scheduled Completion	Actual Completion
1. Foundation completed	August 5	August 2
2. Framing completed	August 10	August 7
3. Exterior finished	August 25	
4. Electrical wiring completed	August 20	
5. Heating and A/C installed	August 25	
6. Interior finished	September 22	

Budget Control Charts

Budget control charts are generally of two varieties. One lists the project steps or subunits with actual costs compared to budget. It's similar to project control charts, which were discussed earlier, and can be generated by hand or computer. The other kind is a graph of budgeted costs compared to actual. Either bar or line graphs may be used. Bar graphs usually relate budgeted and actual costs by project steps, while line graphs usually relate planned cumulative project costs to actual costs over time.

Project management software can produce a budget control chart from data you enter into the application.

Example of a Budget Control Chart

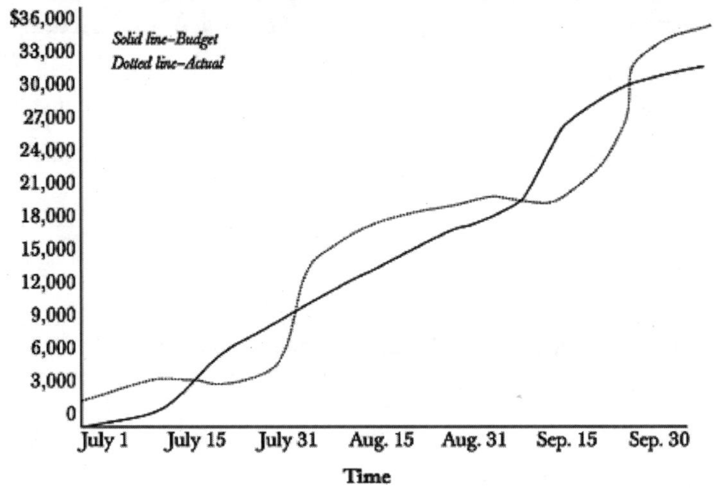

Another helpful approach to budget control is to compare the percentage of budget spent to the percentage of project completed. The data can be compared by making a list or a graph. While the percentage of budget spent is a precise figure, the percentage of project completed should be estimated by someone familiar with the project and its progress.

Monitoring Performance

The heart of the control process is monitoring work in progress. It's your way to know what's going on—how actual compares to plan. With effective monitoring, you know if and when corrective action is required. Following are ways to keep abreast of project progress:

Inspection is probably the most common way to monitor project performance. It's handled by trained inspectors as well as by the project manager. Get out into the area where the work is being performed and observe what's going on. Inspection is an effective way to see whether project specifications are being met, as well as whether there's unnecessary waste or unsafe work practices. Inspections should be unannounced and on a random schedule. However, they should also be open and direct. Ask questions and listen to explanations.

Interim progress reviews are communications between the project manager and those responsible for the various steps of a project. Progress reviews can be in a group or on an individual basis, and either face-to-face or by telephone. Alternatively, progress reports can be submitted in writing. Progress reviews typically occur on a fixed time schedule—daily or weekly—or are keyed to the completion of individual project steps. These scheduled reviews are typically augmented by reviews called by either the project manager or the one responsible for the work. (Guidelines for conducting progress reviews follow.)

Testing is another way to verify project quality. Certain tests are usually written into the specifications to confirm that the desired quality is being achieved. Typical tests include pressure or stress tests on mechanical components.

Auditing can be done during the course of a project or at its conclusion. Common areas for audit are financial record-keeping, purchasing practices, safety practices, security practices, maintenance procedures, and authority for disbursement. Auditors should be experts in the area of the project under review and, typically, aren't members of the project team. After carefully examining the area under review, a report is written describing in detail what was found and pointing out practices that deviate from established policy, authorized procedures, or sound business practices.

Effective monitoring includes more than one source of information. In addition to data from records, a combination of inspections, progress reviews, testing, and auditing will round out your information and keep you up to date on the status of your project.

Conducting Interim Progress Reviews

Interim progress reviews typically occur on a fixed time schedule, for example, daily or weekly. They also may occur when some problem is observed or at the completion of a significant step. Three topics are usually on the agenda:

- Review progress against plan
- Review problems encountered and how they were handled
- Review anticipated problems with proposed plans for handling them

The project manager's role during an interim progress review is to achieve the objectives of knowing the status of operations and influencing the course of future events, as necessary. During the discussion, the project manager may take on any of the following roles:

Listener

Listen as an individual updates you on progress, deviation from plan, problems encountered, and solutions proposed. Listen not only to what's said, but also how it's said. Is the person excited, frustrated, discouraged? Help clarify what's being said by asking questions, and verify what you think is being said by restating your understanding of both facts and feelings.

Contributor

In many interim reviews, progress is in line with plans. However, you occasionally will have problems to deal with. When this occurs, you can contribute to their solution by directing the other person toward possible courses of action. Use your knowledge and experience as necessary to move the project forward.

Integrator

An important role of a project manager is to integrate the individual parts of a project into a compatible whole. Is something being neglected? Is there a duplication of effort? How can available resources be best deployed?

Leader

Perhaps the most important role for the project manager is that of leader. Through a variety of techniques, you must keep the team's effort directed toward the common goal of completing the project according to specifications, on time, and within budget. You must confirm and recognize good performance, correct poor performance, and keep interest and enthusiasm high.

Taking Corrective Action

As you monitor project performance, there will be times when actual doesn't measure up to plan. Such occasions call for corrective action. But don't be too quick to take action. Some deficiencies are self-correcting. It's unrealistic to expect consistent progress each day. Sometimes you fall behind, and sometimes you're ahead, but in a well-planned project, you'll probably finish on schedule and within budget.

When quality isn't according to specification, the customary action is to do it over according to plan. However, this needs to be more closely examined in some instances. For example, if the work or material exceeds specifications, you may choose to accept it. If it falls short, you need to consider how much it deviates from specifications and whether the deficiency will cause the project to fail its performance evaluation. The final decision may be to have the work redone.

When the project begins to fall behind schedule, there are three alternatives that may correct the problem. The first is to examine the work remaining to be done and decide whether the lost time can be recovered in the next steps. If this isn't feasible, consider offering an incentive for on-time completion of the project. The incentive could be justified if you compare this expenditure to potential losses due to late completion. Finally, consider deploying more resources. This, too, will cost more but may offset further losses from delayed completion.

When the project begins to exceed budget, consider the work remaining and whether or not cost overruns can be recouped on work yet to be completed. If this isn't practical, consider narrowing the project scope or obtaining more funding.

TAKING CORRECTIVE ACTION

Summarize three examples in which you were required to take corrective action and how well you handled each one.

What to Do When You Start Falling Behind

The checks (✓) in the **Cost** and **Schedule** columns indicate actions that could be effective in dealing with these parameters.

	Action	Cost	Schedule
1.	**Renegotiate**. Discuss with your client the prospect of increasing the budget or extending the deadline.	✓	✓
2.	**Recover during later steps**. If you begin to fall behind in the early steps of a project, look at later steps. Perhaps you can save on later steps so the overall budget and/or schedule will be met.	✓	✓
3.	**Narrow project scope.** Perhaps nonessential elements of the project can be eliminated, thereby reducing costs and/or saving time.	✓	✓
4.	**Deploy more resources**. You may need to put more people or machines on the project to meet a critical schedule. Increased costs must be weighed against the importance of the deadline.		✓
5.	**Accept substitution**. When something isn't available or is expensive, substituting a comparable item may solve your problem.	✓	✓
6.	**Seek alternative sources**. When a supplier can't deliver within budget or schedule, look for others who can. (You may choose to accept a substitute rather than seek other sources.)	✓	✓
7.	**Accept partial delivery**. Sometimes a supplier can deliver a partial order to keep your project on schedule and complete the delivery later.		✓
8.	**Offer incentives**. Go beyond the scope of the original contract and offer a bonus or other incentive for on-time delivery.		✓
9.	**Demand compliance**. Sometimes demanding that people do what they agreed to do gets the desired results. You may have to appeal to higher management for backing and support.	✓	✓

Providing Feedback

Project managers can find many opportunities to provide feedback to those who have a hand in completing a project. Through feedback, individuals learn about the effect their behavior has on others and on the project's success. Feedback serves to maintain good performance and correct poor performance. To be effective, however, it must be handled properly. This illustration shows the continuous loop that exists when there's good feedback.

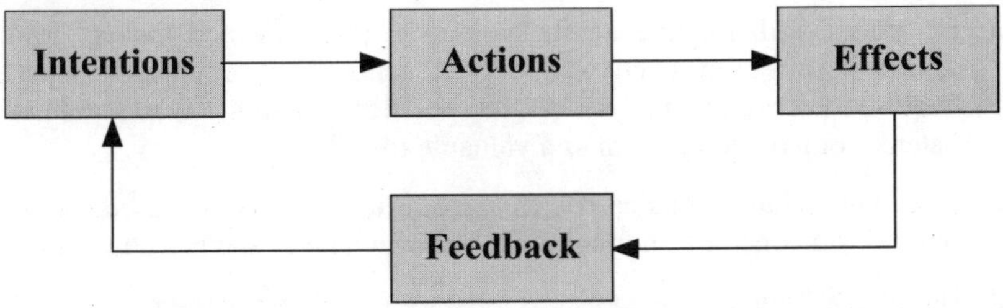

The most important guideline when providing feedback is to deal only with what you can observe. This limits your conversation to actions and results, because you can't observe someone's intentions.

When offering positive feedback, describe the actions and results in a straightforward way and include an appropriate statement of your reaction. For example, you might tell someone, "By staying late last night and finishing the work you were doing, the project was able to move forward on schedule. I appreciate your putting out the extra effort."

Negative feedback can be handled in the same manner, but an important element is missing, which is how the team member should deal with similar situations in the future. The following sequence should prove more effective.

Handling negative feedback

- Describe the observed actions and results. Ask the individual if those were his or her intended results.
- With a typical "No" response, ask what different actions would likely produce the desired results.
- Discuss alternative courses of action.
- Agree upon a way to handle similar situations if they should occur in the future.

Check Your Feedback Style

Rate yourself by placing a check in front of each action that's typical of how you handle giving feedback. The ones you don't check represent opportunities for development.

- ❑ Describe rather than evaluate. By describing observed action and results, the individual is free to use or not use the information. By avoiding evaluation, you reduce the likelihood of a defensive reaction.
- ❑ Be specific rather than general. Avoid using "always" and "never." Rather, discuss specific times and events. Avoid generalized conclusions, such as, "you're too dominating." Rather, be specific by saying, "When you don't listen to others, you may miss a valuable idea."
- ❑ Deal with behavior that can be changed. Frustration is increased when you remind someone of a shortcoming over which he or she has no control.
- ❑ Be timely. Generally, feedback is most useful at the earliest opportunity after the behavior.
- ❑ Communicate clearly. This is particularly important when handling negative feedback. One way to ensure clear communication is to have the receiver rephrase the feedback to see if it corresponds with what you had in mind.

PROVIDING FEEDBACK

Summarize three examples in which you were required to provide feedback and how well you handled each one.

Negotiating for Resources

Negotiating for resources—materials, supplies, and services—is an important process that takes up as much as 20% of a manager's time. Negotiating is a way to resolve differences, and, as such, it can contribute significantly to the success of your project.

Negotiating is best understood when viewed as a process of communications. This approach clarifies your roles of communicator and listener—both of which must be successfully carried out to achieve your goal in the negotiations.

Problems encountered in negotiations can usually be attributed to the approach taken by either one or both of the parties to the process. You need to recognize and be responsive to the attitudes and actions that influence the way people respond to each. These factors are keys to resolving difficulties experienced in the negotiation process.

Even with all its challenges, negotiation remains the best way to coordinate interests and resolve differences between people. It's the only process that allows people with different perspectives and priorities to work them out peacefully and anticipate a mutually beneficial outcome.

The ideas presented here will prepare you to negotiate effectively.

Negotiation

Negotiation is a discussion between two parties with a goal of reaching agreement on issues that separate them when neither party has the power (or the desire to use its power) to force an outcome.

Ten Guidelines for Effective Negotiation

1 **Prepare.** Do your homework. Know what outcome you want and why. Find out what outcome the other party wants. Avoid negotiating when you aren't prepared—ask for the time you need. As part of your preparation, figure out what you'll do if you're unable to come to an agreement. Your power in negotiation develops from attractive alternatives—the greater your ability to walk away, the stronger your bargaining position.

2 **Minimize perceptual differences.** The way you see something can be quite different from how the other party sees it. Don't assume you know the other person's view. Ask questions to gain understanding and restate your understanding, so it can be confirmed or corrected by the other party.

3 **Listen.** Active, attentive listening is mandatory to effective negotiation. Let the other side have an equal share of the airtime. (If you're talking more than 50% of the time, you aren't listening enough.) In the process, respect silence. Occasionally, people need to collect their thoughts before moving ahead. Don't try to fill this time with talking.

4 **Take notes.** You need to know where you are—what has been agreed to and what remains to be resolved. Don't rely on memory. Take notes and then summarize your agreement in a memorandum.

5 **Be creative.** Early closure and criticism stifle creative thinking. Be willing to set some time aside to explore different and unusual ways to solve your problem. During this time, don't permit criticism of the ideas offered. All negotiations can benefit from nonjudgmental creative thinking.

6 **Help the other party.** Good negotiators recognize that the other party's problem is their problem as well. Put yourself in the other's position and work to find a solution that meets everyone's needs. After all, no agreement will hold up unless both parties support it.

7 **Make good trade-offs.** Avoid giving something for nothing. At least get some goodwill or an obligation for future payback. The basic principle to follow is to trade what's cheap to you but valuable to the other party for what's valuable to you but cheap to the other party.

8 **Be quick to apologize.** An apology is the quickest, surest way to de-escalate negative feelings. It needn't be a personal apology. An apology for the situation you're in can be just as effective. Also, don't contribute to a problem by making hostile remarks. Hostility takes the discussion away from the issues and shifts it to a defense of self, where the goal is to destroy the opponent.

9 **Avoid ultimatums.** An ultimatum requires the other party to either surrender or fight. Neither outcome will contribute to future cooperation. Avoid boxing someone in. This happens when you offer only two alternatives, neither of which is desirable to the other person.

10 **Set realistic deadlines.** Many negotiations continue too long because no deadline exists. A deadline requires both sides to be economical in their use of time. It permits you to question the value of certain discussion topics and encourages both sides to consider concessions and trade-offs in order to meet deadlines.

"But, Og, if we keep clubbing each other, we'll never finish the cave."

Resolving Differences

What's best for one department or group isn't necessarily best for others. Out of these differences can come creative solutions when the situation is handled properly. Skill in resolving differences is an important quality for successful project managers.

Differences can be resolved my way, your way, or our way. As a result, four strategies emerge:

- Demanding
- Problem solving
- Bargaining
- Giving in

The strategy one chooses to resolve differences tends to result from an interplay of assertiveness and cooperation. This process can be clouded by emotion at times, and it's difficult to achieve a satisfactory outcome when this happens. Therefore, when you sense that either the other person's or your thinking is clouded by emotion, ask to delay discussion for a while. The following issues influence assertiveness and cooperation.

Assertiveness

- People tend to be more assertive when an issue is important to them.
- People tend to be more assertive when they're confident of their knowledge.
- People tend to be more assertive when things are going against them.
- People tend to be less assertive when they feel they're at a power disadvantage.

Cooperation

- People tend to be more cooperative when they respect the other person.
- People tend to be more cooperative when they value the relationship.
- People tend to be more cooperative when they're dependent on the other person to help carry out the decision.

Strategies for Resolving Differences

Given the interplay of assertiveness and cooperation, the following strategies are common for resolving differences.

Demanding

Demanding means high in assertiveness and low in cooperation. It suggests confidence and that the issue is important, coupled with a lack of concern for the relationship and no dependency on the other person.

Problem Solving

Problem solving means high in assertiveness, coupled with high cooperation. It suggests that the issue is important and that there's the need for an ongoing relationship with the other person.

Bargaining

Bargaining is moderate in both assertiveness and cooperation. It suggests that an important issue is being addressed by equally powerful parties. Each must be willing to give a little to reach agreement. Bargaining is also an appropriate backup strategy when joint problem solving seems unattainable.

Giving In

Giving in is low in assertiveness and high in cooperation. The issue may be unimportant to you, you may lack knowledge, or you may simply want to go along with the other person's proposal in order to build up the relationship between you.

Each strategy has its place. However, too few people recognize the conditions that support each strategy. Many people adopt one approach for resolving differences and use it in all situations. Obviously, it will be ineffective in many cases. Learn to distinguish among the various types of situations and, in each one, adopt an approach that has the greatest chance of success in the long run. Don't overlook the importance of maintaining cooperative relationships.

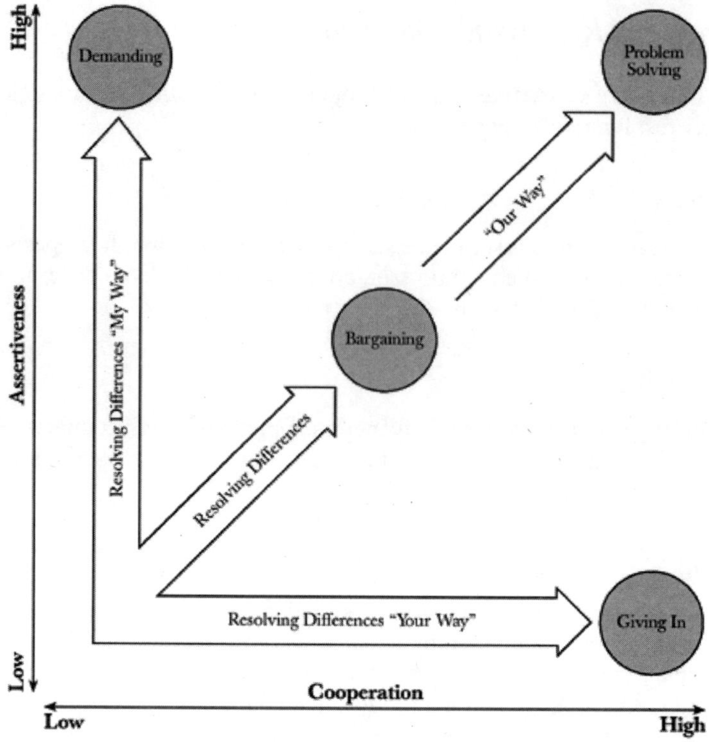

Assertiveness vs. Cooperation

Common Sources of Differences in Project Management

- Allocation of human resources. With limited personnel, project managers often have views different from those of others on how staff are assigned.
- Use of equipment and facilities. Project managers often differ with others over the use of equipment and facilities that must be shared.
- Costs. As you work at controlling costs against the approved project budget, you often encounter conflict with suppliers who feel a need to increase costs over their original commitment.
- Technical opinions. Frequently there are different opinions on how something ought to be done.
- Administrative procedures. Administrative procedures often become points of difference, especially when not followed.
- Responsibilities. There are occasions when more than one person claims an area of responsibility and other occasions when no one wants to accept responsibility.
- Scheduling. Differences develop around schedules and deadlines. And others you depend on may not deliver on their commitments.
- Priorities. There may be differences about which things are more important and, therefore, which should be handled first.

HANDLING DIFFERENCES

What kinds of differences have you observed on projects? Were they handled well? If no, how could they have been handled differently?

____

____

____

____

____

____

____

____

Communicating

Communication skills permeate the entire process of project management. Successful project managers communicate effectively with their clients, team members, and those upon whom they depend for goods and services. As a project manager, you must share information, establish clear expectations, and build a group of people into a smooth-functioning team.

Effective communication in face-to-face settings, on the telephone, and by email is inherent to the skillful use of delegation, feedback, and negotiation. Each of these ideas is addressed at various points in this book, but it's worthwhile here to mention the importance of the most basic communication skill—listening. Your success, and the success of the project, depends on your ability to listen—and hear—what's being said, as well what *isn't* being said, by all participants.

Listening Skills

It's just as important for you to understand what others are telling you as it is for you to be understood. But this is no easy task. Hearing isn't listening. Listening isn't understanding. Listening depends on hearing and leads to understanding. It's the process of taking in information and synthesizing it into something that's understood.

Understanding grows from good listening. What someone doesn't say, or avoids saying, often is more important to full understanding than what is said. To be a fully effective listener, you must be both physically and intellectually engaged in the process.

The activity on the following page will help you assess your listening skills. Complete it carefully and honestly. The results will help you determine where you should focus your energies to improve your communication skills and achieve better results with your project team.

ASSESS YOUR LISTENING SKILLS

Place a check next to the statements you believe you've mastered.

- ❑ When someone asks me something that I don't fully understand, I ask for clarification.
- ❑ I typically pay close attention when talking with someone.
- ❑ I listen for meaning rather than just words.
- ❑ I never pretend to listen when I'm not.
- ❑ I'm careful to distinguish between inference and fact.
- ❑ I don't allow my feelings about a subject to interfere with hearing what someone has to say.
- ❑ I don't let emotion-laden words arouse antagonism.
- ❑ I don't tune people out because the subject they're talking about isn't interesting to me.
- ❑ I try to identify my purpose for listening to someone.
- ❑ I don't listen primarily for facts.
- ❑ I listen for what's being left out.
- ❑ I maintain comfortable eye contact with the person I'm talking with.
- ❑ I'm relaxed but attentive during discussions.
- ❑ I listen to how something is said as well as listening to what's said.
- ❑ I pay attention to nonverbal behavior.
- ❑ I check for understanding of what's said rather than assume I understand.
- ❑ I avoid making absolute statements.

How can you improve as a listener? ______________________________

____

____

____

Tips for Becoming a Better Communicator

- ▶ Pay attention when someone talks to you. Focus your attention and energy on listening.
- ▶ Maintain eye contact during discussions.
- ▶ Concentrate on what's said. Don't be distracted by appearance, style, or mannerisms.
- ▶ Verify your understanding of what you're told through questions and summaries.
- ▶ Avoid slang, jargon, and acronyms unless you know they'll be understood.
- ▶ Check your understanding of what you see rather than assuming or drawing incorrect inferences.
- ▶ Maintain a tentativeness in your conclusions rather than taking a dogmatic position.
- ▶ Be cautious about blaming or judging others. Check your facts and state your position, then examine any differences in perception.
- ▶ When something goes wrong, treat it as an opportunity to improve in the future rather than expending energy identifying who's at fault.
- ▶ Use "I" statements to describe how you see things rather than "you" statements, which can seem judgmental and threatening.
- ▶ Use pronouns carefully. You communicate much more clearly when you refer to someone or something by name rather than by "he," "she," or "it."
- ▶ Stay with a topic long enough to develop full understanding rather than flitting from topic to topic.
- ▶ Be willing to set your topic aside until the other person's has been discussed. Then return to yours.
- ▶ Use broad questions to open discussions and gain information. For example, you might ask, "How are things going?" rather than, "Have you finished that report yet?"

Part Summary

In this part, you learned how to coordinate the **implementation** phase. You learned how to establish **standards** to **control** work in progress, how to monitor **performance**, and how to take **corrective action**. Next, you learned how to provide **feedback** to those involved in a project, and learned how to use ten guidelines for effective **negotiation**. You learned how to **resolve differences**. Finally, you learned how to use **listening skills** and other techniques to communicate effectively.

PART 5

Completing the Project

> *"A project is complete when it starts working for you, rather than you working for it."*
>
> **–Scott Allen**

In this part:

- Bringing the Project to a Successful Conclusion
- Project Management in a Nutshell

Bringing the Project to a Successful Conclusion

The goal of project management is to obtain client acceptance of the project's end result. This means that the client agrees that the quality specifications of the project parameters were met. In order to have the acceptance stage go smoothly, the client and project manager must have well-documented criteria for judging performance in place from the beginning of the project. This isn't to say that the criteria haven't changed since project inception. However, when changes were made, the contract should have been amended to list specification changes, along with any resulting changes in schedule and budget.

Objective, measurable criteria are always best, while subjective criteria are risky and subject to interpretation. There should be no room for doubt or ambiguity, although this standard is often difficult to achieve. It's also important to be clear about what the project output is expected to accomplish. For instance, the following three outcomes may produce entirely different results: the product performs the specified functions; it was built according to approved design; or it solves the client's problem.

The project may or may not be complete when results are delivered to the client. Often there are documentation requirements, such as operation manuals, completed drawings, and a final report, that still have to be provided. Staff may need to be trained to operate the new facility or product, and a final audit is common.

Finally, project team members need to be reassigned; surplus equipment, materials, and supplies disposed of; and facilities released.

The final step of any project should be an evaluation review. This is a look back over the project to see what was learned that will contribute to the success of future projects. This review is best done by the core project team and typically in a group discussion.

A Successful Project

A successful project is one that's completed on schedule and within budget and meets quality specifications.

Project Completion Checklist

- ❑ Test project output to see that it works.
- ❑ Write operations manual.
- ❑ Complete final drawings.
- ❑ Deliver project output to client.
- ❑ Train client's personnel to operate project output.
- ❑ Reassign project personnel.
- ❑ Dispose of surplus equipment, materials, and supplies.
- ❑ Release facilities.
- ❑ Summarize major problems encountered and their solutions.
- ❑ Document technological advances made.
- ❑ Summarize recommendations for future research and development.
- ❑ Summarize lessons learned in dealing with interfaces.
- ❑ Write performance evaluation reports on all project staff.
- ❑ Provide feedback on performance to all project staff.
- ❑ Complete final audit.
- ❑ Write final report.
- ❑ Conduct project review with upper management.
- ❑ Declare the project complete.

PROJECT EVALUATION FORM

1. How close to scheduled completion was the project's actual completion?

____

____

2. What did you learn about scheduling that will help on the next project?

____

____

____

3. How close to budget was the final cost?

____

____

4. What did you learn about budgeting that will help on the next project?

____

____

____

5. Upon completion, did the project output meet client specifications?

____

____

6. If additional work was required, please describe:

____

____

____

7. What did you learn about writing specifications that will help on the next project?

____

____

____

CONTINUED

CONTINUED

8. What did you learn about staffing that will help on the next project?

____

____

____

9. What did you learn about monitoring performance that will help on the next project?

____

____

____

10. What did you learn about taking corrective action that will help on the next project?

____

____

____

11. What technological advances were made on this project?

____

____

____

12. What tools and techniques were developed that will be useful on the next project?

____

____

____

13. What recommendations do you have for future research and development?

____

____

____

CONTINUED

CONTINUED

14. What lessons did you learn from dealings with service organizations and outside vendors?

____

____

____

15. If you had the opportunity to do the project over, what would you do differently?

____

____

____

Project Manager's Checklist

- ❑ Define the project
- ❑ Select a strategy
- ❑ Develop specifications
- ❑ Develop a schedule
- ❑ Develop a budget
- ❑ Organize the project team
- ❑ Assign duties and responsibilities
- ❑ Train new team members
- ❑ Monitor progress
- ❑ Take corrective action
- ❑ Provide feedback
- ❑ Test final outcome
- ❑ Deliver outcome to client
- ❑ Write operations manual
- ❑ Train client personnel
- ❑ Reassign project staff
- ❑ Dispose of surplus equipment, materials, and supplies
- ❑ Release facilities
- ❑ Evaluate project performance
- ❑ Complete final audit
- ❑ Complete project report
- ❑ Review project with management

RATE YOURSELF AS A PROJECT MANAGER

Rate yourself on each of the following skills required to be a successful project manager. Place a check (✓) next to the skill you feel confident about. When you're finished, those that aren't checked represent opportunities for your development.

My current project management skills include:

- ❑ Organizing a project from beginning to end.
- ❑ Structuring a plan that will stand up under pressure.
- ❑ Getting people to accept my plan and support it.
- ❑ Setting measurable project objectives.
- ❑ Motivating team members.
- ❑ Helping team members solve problems.
- ❑ Utilizing available resources.
- ❑ Eliminating waste of time and money.
- ❑ Measuring project performance.
- ❑ Using information systems that respond to project needs.
- ❑ Communicating with everyone involved in the project.
- ❑ Listening to what others have to say.

Project Management in a Nutshell

Projects are temporary undertakings that have a definite beginning and end. This feature distinguishes them from the ongoing work of an organization. There are four phases in any successful project: defining, planning, implementing, and completing. The diagram shown on the next page summarizes these phases.

It's imperative to the success of a project that it be clearly defined before it's undertaken. Any definition should include the criteria for determining successful completion of the project. It's reasonable to expect changes to occur once the project is under way, but these changes should be documented along with any resulting impact on schedule and budget.

A successful project produces an outcome that performs as expected, by deadline, and within cost limits. Thus, the three parameters by which a project is planned and controlled are established. Quality is defined by specifications, time is defined by schedule, and costs are defined by budget.

To carry out the work of the project, a temporary team is usually assembled. This necessitates developing an organization, assigning duties and responsibilities, and training people in their duties. Frequently, policies and procedures are required to clarify how the team is to function during the project.

When work on the project begins, the project manager has many responsibilities. The efforts of various individuals and groups must be coordinated so that things run smoothly, and the progress of the project must be monitored and measured against plans. When deviations occur, corrective action must be taken. Also, project managers are expected to provide feedback to team members, negotiate for materials, supplies, and service, and help resolve differences that occur.

The goal of a project is to deliver an outcome to the client. When that day finally arrives, there are still things to be done before the project is complete. These can include writing operations manuals, training client personnel to use the project output, reassigning project personnel, disposing of surplus equipment, materials, and supplies, evaluating the experience, completing a final audit, writing a project report, and conducting a project review with upper management.

Not every project requires the same attention to each of these activities. What needs to be done depends upon the type of project you are undertaking, its size and scope, and the type of organization you're affiliated with. Use your own judgment in selecting the steps important to the success of your project.

Best of luck in the projects you undertake. Success can be yours if you use the concepts presented in this book.

Part Summary

In this part, you learned how to bring a project to a successful **conclusion**. You learned how to use a **completion checklist**, and how to **evaluate** a completed project. Finally, you learned how to **rate yourself** as a project manager.

APPENDIX

Appendix to Part 1

Comments & Suggested Responses

Project Management Concepts

1. True
2. True
3. False
4. True
5. True
6. False
7. False
8. False
9. False
10. False
11. False
12. True

Viva-Crisp 50-Minute
Titles in the Series

ISBN	Author	Title	YOP	Price
9788130918174	Gambino	**50 Minutes to Better Software Demos**: *Apply Your Sales Skills with Confidence*	2011	195.00
9788130918488	Bozek	**50 One-Minute Tips to Better Communications**: *Speak, Write and Present More Effectively, 3/e*	2011	250.00
9788130918211	Conlow & Watsabaugh	**Achieving Supervisory Excellence**: *Be the Leader Your People Need*	2011	195.00
9788130918396	McKnight & Chapman	**Attitude**: *Protect Your Most Priceless Asset, 5/e*	2011	245.00
9788130918495	Terry Dickey	**Basics of Budgeting**: *Become a Better Business Planner, 2/e*	2011	250.00
9788130918310	Conlow & Watsabaugh	**Become a Successful Supervisor**: *Develop Essential People Skills*	2011	225.00
9788130918327	Brock	**Better Business Writing**: *Become A More Powerful Communicator, 5/e*	2011	225.00
9788130918228	Dupont	**Business Etiquette & Professionalism**: *Conduct Yourself With Confidence, 3/e*	2011	195.00
9788130918181	Morgan	**Calming Upset Customers**: *Stay in Control ... In any Situation, 4/e*	2011	195.00
9788130918198	Minor	**Coaching and Counseling**: *Become a Better Manager Through Mentoring, 4/e*	2011	195.00
9788130918273	Decker	**Communication Skills for Leaders**: *Deliver a Clear and Consistent Message, 4/e*	2011	225.00
9788130918143	Kindler	**Conflict Management**: *Resolve Disagreement at Work, 4/e*	2011	165.00
9788130918280	Conlow & Watsabaugh	**Creating a High Performance Team**: *Gain the Skills of Today's Successful Leaders*	2011	225.00
9788130918334	Feldman	**Critical Thinking**: *Make Strategic Decisions With Confidence, 2/e*	2011	225.00
9788130918426	Flynn	**E-Mail Management**: *Keep Your Inbox Under Control, 2/e*	2011	245.00
9788130918471	Kravitz & Schubert	**Emotional Intelligence Works**: *Think, Be and Work Smarter, 3/e*	2011	245.00
9788130918150	Maddux	**Ethics in Business**: *Manage With Authority and Fairness, 2/e*	2011	195.00
9788130918235	Rouillard	**Goals and Goal Setting**: *Achieve Measurable Results, 4/e*	2011	195.00
9788130918204	Conlow Watsabaugh	**Handling Difficult People and Situations**: *Lead People Through Adversity*	2011	195.00

ISBN	Author	Title	YOP	Price
9788130918433	Wendover	**High Performance Hiring**: *Select the Best Every Time, 3/e*	2011	245.00
9788130918402	Shea	**Making the Most of Being Mentored**: *Mentors Help Mentees Do, 2/e*	2011	245.00
9788130918242	Scott	**Managing Personal Change**: *Stay Positive and Stay in Control, 3/e*	2011	195.00
9788130918341	Haynes	**Meeting Skills for Leaders**: *Make Meetings More Productive, 4/e*	2011	225.00
9788130918440	Shea	**Mentoring**: *Make It A Mutually Rewarding Experience, 4/e*	2011	245.00
9788130918525	Shandler	**Motivating the Millennial Knowledge Worker**: *Help Today's Workforce Succeed in Today's Economy*	2011	395.00
9788130918167	Mandel	**Presentation Skills**: *Captivate and Educate Your Audience, 4/e*	2011	195.00
9788130918518	Pokras	**Problem Solving for Teams**: *Make Consensus More Achievable, 3/e*	2011	295.00
9788130918259	Haynes	**Project Management**: *Get from the Idea to Implementation Successfully, 4/e*	2011	195.00
9788130918372	Martin	**Quality Customer Service**: *Satisfy Customers–It's Everybody's Job, 5/e*	2011	245.00
9788130918457	Lightle & Doucet	**Sexual Harassment in the Workplace**: *Create a Better Workplace For Everyone, 3/e*	2011	245.00
9788130918501	Lengefeld	**Study Skills Strategies**: *Get the Most From Every Minute of Learning, 4/e*	2011	250.00
9788130918358	Conlow & Watsabaugh	**SuperSTAR Customer Service**: *It's all about C.A.R.E.*	2011	225.00
9788130918297	Maddux & Wingfield	**Team Building**: *Turn Personal Strengths Into Group Success, 5/e*	2011	225.00
9788130918464	Finch	**Telephone Courtesy & Customer Service**: *Be Your Company's Lifeline to Customers, 4/e*	2011	245.00
9788130918389	Conlow & Watsabaugh	**Telephone Skills that Satisfy Customers**: *Unleash the Full Potential of the Telephone*	2011	245.00
9788130918303	Romero	**The Business of Listening**: *Become a More Effective Listener, 4/e*	2011	225.00
9788130918365	Chapman & McKnight	**The New Supervisor**: *Lead With Confidence, 5/e*	2011	225.00
9788130918266	Haynes	**Time Management**: *Get An Extra Day a Week*	2011	195.00
9788130918419	Gill & Chatton	**Understanding Financial Statements**: *Master the Tools That Help You Succeed, 3/e*	2011	245.00